Don't Live to Die But Live to Love

Stephanie M. Massey

ROYAL MEDIA
AND PUBLISHING LLC

Royal Media and Publishing
P. O. Box 4321
Jeffersonville, IN 47131
502-802-5385
http://royamediaandpublishing.com
royalmediapublishing@gmail.com

Cover Design: Bill Lacy Designs

ISBN-13: 978-1543006506
ISBN-10: 1543006507

Printed in the United States of America

John 1:9 – If we confess our sins, He faithful and just to forgive us our sins and to cleanse us from (evil) all unrighteousness.

Proverb 24:16 – For a righteous man may fall seven times and rise again, but the wicked shall fall by calamity.

Samuel 12:1-23 – Give praises unto the Lord when death is upon, for you cannot bring them back. The rich man poor man story. Have faith and understand the wages of sin. Sin does not fall upon you…sin maybe upon someone very close to you.

John – For I love so, I am very careful as to the mistakes and sins I commit. The Lord is my shepherd and I shall not want. Thank you Jesus….

The Criswell Morning

Good Morning, World

I am grateful to have awoken to you.

Today, I choose to live better than yesterday. If I have made any enemies, I ask that the universe will forgive me. During the path of today, I will have connected them and we will love one another as we should.

Today is the day the Lord has made and let us dwell in it and be productive. IN JESUS NAME, THAT HOLY NAME OF JESUS...AMEN!!!!

Michael & Ronnell – Lord, may you please bestow peace and understanding upon these today. Let Reuben feel my love and your presence.

Table of Contents

Letter from the
Author

Chapter 1	Where I Am with God	1
Chapter 2	When You Talk About Love	7
Chapter 3	God Loves Us & Looks at Our Hearts	13
Chapter 4	Feeling Needed	21
Chapter 5	Group Process/Correctional Recovery	33
Chapter 6	A Letter from the VP of the United States	41
Chapter 7	Dear God	43
Chapter 8	Dear Father	45
Chapter 9	Not Knowing How or When to Let Go	83
Chapter 10	I Was Not Built to Break	93
Chapter 11	Good Morning World	103
Chapter 12	In My Last Days	135
Chapter 13	My Love Letter to God	149
Chapter 14	Death	151

Chapter 1

Where I Am with God

See where I am with God is helping people to love God, love yourself and to love everyone the way you love yourself.

This is all God ask of us, this is so simple. People go out of their way hurting God trying to love Him. He has done all that He is going to do for us and that's when He died on the cross.

Having faith and believing in all He has asked of us, it makes our lives worth living. He extends His grace and mercy upon our lives. When you know after receiving God through your personal experience, you begin to feel Him. You know that He dwells inside of us because He is a living God. He is inside of you and the only way that you will be able to access Him and utilize His power is to connect with Him.

You got to be able to talk to Him like He is your best friend. Tell Him everything. Yes,

He is God and He supposed to already know- trust me- He do know but He wants you to confess it with your mouth and it's then that He will change your situation. Yeah, I just told you that God has done all He is going to do for you when He died for us on Calvary – trust me- that's true to but by you trusting and believing in Him through you-you have accessed His power to do and be whatever you want to do.

He will then trust enough in you to open your own doors to success. It's not going to rain open hundred-dollar bill, but He has this way of you blessing yourself. Remember, you can't be greedy. You have to start giving to God. He loves a cheerful giver. You MUST tithe. I can't express it enough. You work hard at work all we praise the Lord that you have a job and strength to perform. It's His grace and mercy that allow you to work His will is that we give Him the small percentage of 10% of your gross income $40 dollars a week seem large of a $400-dollar check, but trust me – in doing so, blessings will over flow your cup and you will see them. Your health will change, family problems will end, and all kinds of blessings will flow.

Remember that you can't afford to look for love in all the wrong places – you will never find it. Love inside yourself and you will find everything you need for you. Okay, I see you're not understanding. Everything starts with you. Once you are loved by you and being receptive, I have nappy hair, I'm fat, my nose is either too big or small, my teeth isn't straight, I wished I had hazel eyes or blue else, things you can get over the counter to help shape your image. Get it comfortable fitted for you – Love on you more but keep that faith with God and finally commit yourself to Love God more all day, every day. If you are in a bad relationship get out of it. This will reflect your image, the way you feel about God, yourself. If you have tried to work it out and it don't work – oh – it's over – don't compete with your mate.

Immediately start dating and having fun. Don't sit around and mope the way they would expect. This is the fun part about your life finding the right mate. I've been through many and still have a lot in me. Remember we are not perfect and we cannot expect for perfect to come to us. Yeah we do tend to want more and better for ourselves in our partners, but then look inside yourself and see if you have these same qualities in return to give. Let your hair down and be your relaxed self and flow with the rhythm of your heart.

My man can look like ET as long as he is good to me. Now you see a lot better. Besides with an ugly man we don't have that much drama – he becomes a home body and everything around the house works.

The majority of the time we look to what our peer groups would think about the type of man we have his looks, his educational back-ground, what kind of family he or she came from, his job or skills don't get me wrong, these are some aspects to have but very crucial to real love if that's what you are looking for.

There is no value to real love and what makes you happy. It's sad to say but the homeless shelters have some of the best men and women looking for a second chance at real love and I say this because I have met so many of them all across this land from city to city. I have not been looking for a mate, but if I was that would be my first visit for dating.

First, you know their situation and this is where you can save a person, build them up, make shared decisions and explore a journey to happiness. Meeting a person in a club, you know you have a party goer and maybe a cheater. Meeting them in church is a big mistake when a relapse come, they run to Jesus in hope to prey on its members. It's hard to deceive God looking for a spouse or widow and for some wanting to be a first lady, which God has not ordained for you.

Only to come in and disrupt a congregation looking at the married Pastor. Do not do that. Please leave them grocery store men alone, they are hungry and looking to find someone to cook for them. The mall shoppers are looking for someone to shop for them with your money – if it came down to them buying them some Jordon's or you a Coach purse, what is it going to be – their Jordon's.

Right now, I just thank God for saving me, preserving me, blessing me and keeping me close to Him and when He is ready for me to settle down with peace – He will place them right there before me. I will then be ready.

Chapter 2

When You Talk About Love

Yeah as Patti LaBelle sings you should be talking about we are Orlando Florida. Oh, Father God just how much we need you to change this world so full of HATEFULNESS.

How we are having to mourn this Orlando Florida tragedy massacre: My heart goes out to them and the rest of the world who are affected by this grief.

AS a LGBT author, transgender and activist, I am Orlando Florida in the midst of this massacre. I stand in lieu of the pain for those families of the love ones that lives ended so young and for the families of those that are fighting for their lives.

Something has got to happen. It's got to get better than this. I am so very grateful that so many people have come together to embrace our LGBT community. If we could just keep this love coming.

By no means was this just out of the clear to happen. This terrorist act of hate that targeted our community was planned and could have been prevented. There were so many cries for help that went unnoticed. His girlfriend could have done more. The FBI should have returned the calls back to the gun shop that first alerted them of him trying to buy body armor. There is just so many unanswered questions that rage our minds and hearts of why this happened. As I sit her in my Los Angeles Hotel writing this, my heart is full of fear. As bad as I would like to be down on Pico or Santa Monica Blvd hanging with my friends, my fear will not let me go out. It's sad but it's true. When I am at home in Nashville, Tennessee I am still in fear of going to the gay bars, afraid that a copycat will appear. This is no way easy to have to live here in America. The supposing, the land of the free.

Since 911, I we've been on so many terror alerts. How is this really happening? Why is it so hard to ban these assault guns here in America? These are war guns and we do not have a war going on in this land.

I look back at all the school shootings, the movie theater and now a gay bar killing more people combined. This has got to stop. We have got to come together for the same purpose. "All Lives Matter."

We can't seem to get a President to say "I have the power and I am going to use it." I'm so sick of this petty talk about the Second Amendment. Lord how many times our Judicial System has violated the fourth, eighth and fourteenth amendments to the United States Constitutions which are for the people and yet our prisons across the land are over filled with inmates because these amendments has been violated by the judicial System and nothing, I mean NOTHING has ever been done about this. Now your rich white Republican of the National Rifle Association (NRA) stands behind the second amendment.

What is next – it's gonna take someone to go up into the NRA and use your own weapons to stop this – that would be another uncaused massacre that could be prevented also.

Come Americans – we can do this as a collective whole. Don't vote for Trump or Clinton unless they confess to ban these guns. Election is November, we have time as a collective whole to make away. Enough is enough. It's not like they can be selling this many assault guns here in America that will outweigh all the lives we have lost to these guns.

Black Churches of America, we hold the power to hold our congregations from the voting polls. You can best believe that we are not getting our hands on any of them because if we did, we would not have endured all we did in the 50's, 60's and 70's when the "KKK" was burning our churches, raping our children and killing our strong black men.

If I sound mad, then yes I am, but I'm not radical. I'm telling the truth from an injured community of LGBT and African American community. I have been hit from both sides.

There is something much more powerful than politics going on here. I look to all the black people with large platforms that refuses to come out and be realistic and tell us in our language to understand why you can't come forward. The majority of you all, we made and this is just a little something you all could come through for us and give back to us. I'm just saying and I know I am speaking for a whole lot of people. Try asking the families of those school killings, the theater shooting and now the Orlando Massacre.

Looking at the news today 06/2/16, Donald Trump is so stupid, he busy running his mouth bringing down America didn't even realize that he was the target for assassination.

The game for Presidency of this country has changed. It started with Obama and just has gotten out of hand.

Hillary done been there three times, two as First Lady with Bill and one with Obama. Yeah, in spite of her experience, she'd be a lot better than Trump with no experience, but she should be held accountable to say this is enough. I will stand for the people and band these guns.

Chapter 3

God Loves Us and Looks at our Hearts

I don't know too many people of my LGBT community that are not loving, kind, supportive, giving, caring and just want to be accepted.

People has looked down upon us for many years for selfish reasons and the main one is denial of their own sexual preference.

It's hard when you're able to come out and just be you. Sometimes it means giving up your love ones just to be free. Some, but not all are going to be receptive. Some may fake it, but eventually the truth will come out.

These people that hates us most are those that wants to come out and is afraid of what their families, friends and co-workers will think. Again, Orland murderer is a prime example. He wanted to come out but after being rejected by a few, then trying to live that double life style and his family traditions just wasn't working for him. But why act out as such. He should have just taken his own life and left a letter. These were innocent people – and my heart and love goes out unconditionally to the families of this massacre. I even have some sympathy for his lost soul for not knowing how to love himself, accept God for who he was. Living such a shell of a life had to be extremely hard for him too.

People can be so cruel and judgmental that cause us to react in dangerous, emotional and mental ways that sometimes become too late to reach out.

I praise God daily, sometimes four and five times a day for my deliverance and transformation from Stephen to Stephanie. It was not easy and yet today it's even harder having to deal with all these transgender issues, especially something as small as having to use the same bathroom.

I remember talking to my professor before this happened, I said the bathroom talk is only something small for something big to happen and then this. When I tell you how I hurt. I just wish God could have shown me.

I know that I serve a wonderful God who sits high and looks low. For every one of those that was murdered, we heard nothing but good things about them. I have no doubt that their hearts were of pure gold. I don't have no hell or heaven to put no one, but I am assured that they all were knocking on Heaven's Door.

So to my community – the key is love, keep on loving people the way you want to be loved. God looks at our heart. Love Him whole hearted and love your neighbor as you love yourself. Even when you feel disrespected and not receptive. Just keep on doing your part.

People will continue to dislike you for who you are and how you openly live your life as lesbians, bi-sexual, gays and transgender people, as long as you are loving you respectfully, acknowledging that there is a high power than you or man and woman and knowing that the spirt of God dwells within you, you are doing your part.

God does not make mistakes when He or She plucks your flower for the Heavenly Garden. The act of murder is of the Satan. God does not kill, so please don't feel some type of way when death comes upon you love ones.

It is never easy, but His comforting will ease the pain when you know you are living for God. Remember God looks within your heart. You have done nothing wrong. For we all live in sin and we are not to judge one another. Judging is just another added sin that we as gay people do not look kindly upon.

Together we shall overcome this with the power of love we will overcome this. We shall not let the hate that was thrown upon us stop us from living our lives. Think of all the love ones that died together in love.

Keep us strong and keep them alive through us.

My prayers will always be with them and their families. They will be especially thought of at this tragic anniversaries, birthdays, other holidays and just being missed.

I just can't get over how curial people can be and especially in the name of God, Allah, Buddhism or just whatever it is you choose to worship. How can one's belief be so conveyed that you can't interpret the word of God with your personal relationship instead of following a traditional belief. Not all traditional beliefs are true and the sad part is that you are in hell following a tradition that was misunderstood.

Everything that God mad is good. He made us out of His own image. In spite of how we live our lives, what we achieve in life whether it's big or small, God is still going to love us whether we are black, white, Hispanic, Iranians or what, underneath our skin out blood is RED the same as Our Savior Jesus Christ.

Whether we are straight, bi-sexual, lesbians, gay or transgender, God still loves us. He created us in His own image.

The Spirt of God still dwells within our bodies. He has not left us. Come on, I'm telling you what God wants you to know. Don't give up we've got to stand for what we believe and treat people the way they need to be treated as human beings. We are not any better than the other. Just because you have a bigger house, a better car, a little higher education – good for you, that means you have more and higher bills than I do. I refuse to stress and worry about how they are paying their bills.

There is too many things going on in the world, right now surrounding us to be entertained in things we cannot control. The one thing that I am so content with is myself is knowing where I am with God. I am at peace with myself. I love my neighbors the way that He instructed us to do and I love Him whole hearted.

He has allowed me to live 51 years and trust me, they have not been easy. I have come through and survived somethings in my life that I can only say that God brought me out and through. Only He could have done this. And oh how I thank You God and I still give you all the praises.

I am a faithful tither, I am able to go out into this vineyard and take His word, feed and bring His people closer to Him. This is what He expects for us to do for him.

Chapter 4

Feeling Needed

Here it is June 20th 2016; I feel really good. I'm here in Indio, California visiting my best friend and his wife and three kids. I just hung up talking to Casey and my husband, whom I never divorced. Keith stopped by her house and he wanted her to call me, how sweet that was of him. I will always love him in my Whitney Houston voice.

I'm here on vacation and just praying that God will watch over me and my loved ones back at home. I talked to Mike G this morning. I talked with Chief from South Central prison, Jeremy called and he needs me and Coco. I haven't heard from him, but I see where I have missed a call from her. I'm a bit worried about that one. She was recently stabbed in prison, but she's doing alright, a little mentally shaken, but some of the inmates there has told me, "Auntie, she got her a couple of sticks in but when she turned around and was able to touch him, she did her thing and shook his butt good." I am trying not to curse in this book, it's going to be hard but the Lord is on my side. He has been so, so, so, good to me and I just can't keep it to myself.

I was inspired to write this book by my Pastor, Pastor Harris at First Baptist Church of South Inglewood. He's young and very, very anointed by God. I just love him and the First Lady. Yesterday was Father's Day and I know he was looking for me and her I am at my favorite place with my favorite people, but thought of him. I will make it home by Sunday.

When he approached me about this book called "Where I am at with God" right now. I immediately thought – this is a good question, but I'm at Church for one of my dearest friends, Thelma's funeral.

Little did my Pastor know that I had already completed a lot of prayers that I had written daily when I was in prison that I wanted to publish in hopes that I may influence men and women that are incarcerated to help them to pray and turn their problems over to God every day and watch the closeness and personal relationship that they could and would develop with GOD.

It's never about what no one else may think of your relationship with God, they could care less because the majority don't have a personal relationship with God, they just fellowship during church services and when that one day out of a week is over they go back to being who they really are, but Mayo Angelo, said it best. "When people show you who they are believe them."

The saying is "How can you love God when you have never seen and can't love your brothers and sisters, whom you can see every day." God is so real and He's been so good to ME.

These are some of my daily prayers from prison. I sincerely pray that each of you will develop your personal relationships with God and let Him use you in ways that you never would have imagined. I use to be this mean and bad person that could fight and would fight real fast. I was angry with a purpose and I didn't know how to cope with it, so I said at the of 40 years old, if I lived to see it, I would give my life back over to God and whatever came out of it was meant to be. I did struggle in my daily walk with Him and these past eleven years has not been easy but it's been worth it. That's a true saying "He never promised us a rose garden." I don't know who said this but it is the best saying I've heard to help me on me on this journey.

There has been a many of times that I just had to talk to God because the very people I helped during a lot of crisis, I could not call from prison, nor did they write, send missing you cards. I had a few loyal friends that wrote, Lou Lou was like every week. We've been friends for over 35 or 40 years. Gloria and Fulvia mostly holidays, but they did write. Shirley by spells. It was just so hard, but God was there every day and night. Prison life is not easy. The sad part looking back now, I was a threat to the political and judicial system. I never committed new crimes, they would just violate me and send me back to prison over and over and over for things like leaving town, somebody had called on me prison four or five times for nothing.

I was bitter at the system and had visualized me walking up into the court room as a terrorist, laying to ambush them one at a time, but now God is with me and I thank Him for saving me and getting me out of harm's way and in a way that I could bring joy, peace and hope to people in the prisons where I would go. I know the law very well and I was always able to help the inmates go back to court and give lots of their time back. I walked from my cell to the library to outside sitting in the sun preparing cases for court from inmates all across the state of Tennessee Prison system and to this day I still do this for inmates.

Knox County Circuit Court turned a simple shoplifting case into a criminal aggravated robbery and it's in plain view but the higher courts have upheld the State and got 20 years on Coco at 85%. This is an outrage and outcry from the judicial system because of Coco's transgender status, they were prejudiced against her. Now it's an outcry from prison because no one will listen and look at the discriminatory language that turned this into a tragedy.

My prayer now is that this book will open many eyes and hearts and will help me in some pro bono help to fight this most illegal and crooked judicial system across this land.

Heavenly Father,

I thank You for all the joy You have given me. I thank You for the paint that I've experienced because each and every time

I've called upon You and You comforted and eased it right on by Lord. I am still grieving my mom and dad because I am dreaming of them too often. My today's daily bread highlighted "Mixed Emotions" Solomon wrote "Even in laughter the heart may sorrow, and the end of my may be grief." (Proverb 14-13); Again, confirmation that I am walking in the light. Father God Your word clearly states that in eternity "there shall be no more pain, no more sorrow, no more death, nor crying." Lord, I am longing for those days.

Please read my prayers.

Heavenly Father right now in Jesus name, I ask that you will bless each of us that are dealing with mixed emotions, missing our love ones and are confused about Your Word Father God, guide us, comfort us and show us in one another how to love, understand without judgment and to encourage and uplift one another in the righteous of Your word.

Lord amongst us there are some that are having to battle with issues that they are afraid to discuss amongst others. Give them the courage to man up and ask for forgiveness so that they may move forward Lord. You know that there are some that use Your word as a shield to hide behind or under the circumstances surrounding their particular situation, but Lord, I know that You know our hearts. I ask that You will bless us accordingly. Teach us our deen according to Your will so that we may all meet in the vineyard and give You glory. Bless our families and our friends Heavenly Father. Bless our finances so that our families won't have to go without because of our situation. Lord, bless the homeless people that are of this world during this cold season. The children that are having to fend for themselves and the women that are being violated. Strengthen us all Lord so that we can all lean upon You to protect us and keep us out of harm's way. Bless the families of those that didn't wake up this morning, those that are not able to dress themselves or pick up Your word and read it. Give them the strength and wisdom Lord to know Your word and just say a mindful "Thank You" Lord for another day. Lord I thank You for my life. I thank You for all these guys that surrounds me. I know You have a divine plan for us all. I thank You for the staff here Lord that keeps order and peace just by their uniforms. Lord I thank You, I thank You for the insulin I'm about to receive, my medications and my food. Lord this is the day You have made and I am going to be glad in it. Bless my words so that they will be pleasing unto You and encouraging and uplifting to others in Jesus name, Amen, amen, amen.

Heavenly Father,

I want to thank You for this new day — January 1st, 2014. A new day and a new year. As I ended yesterday with last year, my circumstance didn't change but my situation did and for this I am so very grateful. The difference is that my circumstance is being incarcerated and my situations is knowing that this too shall pass.

Father God I have no clue as to what You want me to do, but I am willing and trying to please You. I know that I am closer and closer each day Lord. I pray that You will continue to allow me to grow in You and Your Word. Teach me to understand Your Word better. Give the fruit of Your Spirit as I surrender my life in faith and obedience. Teach me to listen with my heart and see with my faith Father God. I want my heart to be in tune with You. In every stage of my life, let it be true; I want my thoughts and words to honor You, to lift You up in everything I do.

Heavenly Father I need You, I need You to bless my mind with beautiful thoughts of You, to increase my wisdom with Your Words and to bless my tongue so that my words will be pleasing unto You and encouraging, up-lifting and comforting to others. Let Your light shine upon me for others to see the illuminations of Your effect and the power in believing and having pure faith in You.

Lord I thank You for the teaching of my self-value, self-worth and having self-esteem. Taking pride in how I love You, love myself and my neighbors. Lord, thank You for first loving me enough to create Jesus just for me, a sinner. Thank You for Your grace and mercy. Father God thank You for my family. I had no choice about it, but You placed me just where You wanted me to be and for this, I am grateful. You have called my mom, my dad, my brother and my sister home with You. Thank You for the time that I had with them here and I look forward to all of us getting together up there to just praise You forever. Lord I thank You for Clare, Bobby, Casey, Lisa, Regina, Lovie, James, Ronnie, Leroy, John, Paul, Lena, Geneva and Jean. Father God, I pray that this will be the year for all of us to celebrate one another. I thank You for Ms. Dorothy and ask that You will bless her with good health and strength. Father God, watch over all my nieces, nephews, uncles, aunts, cousins and friends. I can't name them all, but You know them all in my heart. I love them way more than they will ever know. Bless St. James and all its members and to send them a Pastor that intends to stay forever. Bless First Baptist of South Inglewood and its members. Jones Street Church of Christ, Phyllis, Nuke and her sons. Lord, I just want to thank You and please bless Mike and his family too in Jesus name I pray. Bless Dean Gilbert Lord, in Jesus name I pray. Amen, amen, amen.

Chapter 5

Group Process/Correctional Recovery

Topic – Each One Teach One

This is where each of us brings the awareness of our brother or someone in the community that is slacking but yet don't realize the seriousness of effect that it could later bring about. Awareness's such as:

1. Not being where they need to be a couple of minutes early, then dragging in just in time.

2. Being impulsive, disrespectful, rude, loud or intimidating not knowing that someone in authority is or could be looking.

3. Smoking when you know it's not permitted.

4. Cell mate not contributing to keeping the cell clean and inspection ready at all times.

Just little things that can help the growth and development of one's rehabilitative behaviors.

This goes for beyond this prison. We are obligated to our family, friends and community in which we live in to mentor our younger generations. To teach them at an earlier age the ripple effect of drugs, crimes, prisons, gangs, violence, all these things in which could save one young person from coming to prison or juvenile detentions such as Woodlawn Hills. Imagine the ripple effect of just on juvenile or young adults coming into the system will have on not just himself, but his family, his community, the justice system, the institution then other inmates in which he already knows from the streets that may already be in a gang, influence him, or he end up on the opposite side, just so many people that one person can have a powerful impact on as a ripple effect.

I challenge each one in this group tonight to be a part of the Each One Teach One, to help within and to inspire on the outside. We have the power to change many people lives if we CHOOSE to.

Starting around the circle, each one is to describe the community in which you just left from before being violated and what Each One Teach One could benefit from your imposition as a mentor or leader steeping up to make a change not just for yourself but for your community as a whole.

What are you willing to do?

Would you challenge others to join you by bringing this before your church, parole officer or people on the job?

Ask other family members that has supported you during this trial.

Today – I am upset because of the nasty rumors that are being stated about Bill Cosby. Yes – it don't look good because so many of these hungry desperate women are coming forth only because they're hoping to gain something in the end.

What else could it be – other than to distract America from the Ferguson Missouri Riots that's about to take place tomorrow, if that jury return its ballot not to charge that man with murder.

Those women knew what they were doing back then just as they know what they are doing today. When a man and woman get together in a hotel room and sharing drinks not to mention that there in the presence of an Icon and very wealthy, it just does something for their ego, uplift their self-esteem and the next thing you know they've gave up their bodies perhaps for some, her a shot at fame and most didn't make it and now they are feeling shame.

I am more than sure that had they gone to the authorities the next day and gave their claim of being raped by a black man because all the ones I've seen has been white women – just one District Attorney would have pursued this case in hops for a brighter future.

This is a bunch of bull crap and what happened to innocent until proven guilty. Americans have already found him guilty and convicted him even then though there has not been a trial.

NBC withdrawing his sitcom every black person in America should not support any television events on NBC, I know I will never watch them again. CNN seems to support him being guilty. This still shows racial attacks on him in spite of success.

Unlike Michael Jackson, Bill choose not to give a statement. I would not either and if I did those women would not like it. If he fed into this scandal, it would be blown out of context and somebody, somewhere would capitalize off of it. He's doing the best thing not giving a public account of any of it. It's been proven by one of the desperate women by her own words in her book that this did not happen and she changed her story.

America, wake up. Quit judging others and always assuming the worst to be true.

White America, stop being so radical and quick to convict a person based on their skin color.

Black American men, stay within your lane and race and quit always running to the other side of the fence when your reaches your highest peak in success…look around you are doomed to be brought down…it never fails.

Write down the things that you would like to change about yourself that will make you a better person. After you have written them down, put them into a wine bottle and throw it out to sea. For whoever shall read this, I know that you have found this…please look me up to see how I am doing. My name is Stephanie Michelle Massey. I am 49 years old looking to celebrate my 50th birthday on April 21st 2015.

As of this moment, I am sitting in my prison cell watching Miami whip Denver in this football game and I am cheering for

Payton Manning. They are about to go into half-time.

Tomorrow is my big day. I am going home and I can't wait. I've been down for fifty-three weeks and each one has been very long. I lost my father during my first week, thereafter, I lost a close cousin and numerous friends. In my last month, my favorite aunt Annie died which took a very major toll on my health and I became very sick.

Chapter 6

A letter from the Vice President of the United States

Stephanie M. Massey

#216989

N.W.C.C. Unit 6/27

960 State Route 212

Tiptonville, TN 38079

Dear Stephanie,

Thank you for your message. I truly appreciate your kind words and I value your support.

In a time when our country and our world face many challenges, the President and I are continually energized by the messages of encouragement we receive from people around the Nation. It is a privilege to hear so many diverse voices, ideas and perspectives.

As we continue to work together to strengthen our economy, fund much-needed reforms in our health care and education systems and secure a more peaceful world for our children, we encourage you to remain an active participant in our public discourse. It will take the hope and resolve of people like you to ensure that our Nation's tomorrows are better than our yesterdays.

Thanks again for writing, and I wish you the very best in the days and years ahead.

Sincerely,

Joseph R. Biden, Jr.

Chapter 7

Dear God,

Here it is October 2013, 8 years ago I was so hurt by the loss of my very best friend Ms. Bamp. It doesn't even seem as long. I just pray according to his heart he made it into heaven.

Then there's Annie Ruth, and Darlene whose birthdays to celebrate. As well as Ms. Bamp. I'm sure that she's giving them a beautiful show with Chris & Dee encouraging her as we all did at the Voo. There's Miss Baba, Crystal Blue, Brewser, Dee, Chris, Ms. Bamp, Tony, Patrick and so many more to go from my circle and I feel so blessed to still be here and for this I am so very grateful.

Lord, I just ask that You'll continue to keep my heart and mind regulated on You so that I may never fall aside of my path whereas I can't get up. I ask that You'll give special attention to those that are homeless and hungry. I ask Lord that You will protect those innocent children from abuse and molestation. Be a comforter to the family of those that has lost a love one. Most of all Lord to bless those of us that are in jails & prisons that are still trying to seek you.

Father God, please don't forget those that are in the hospitals and nursing homes. Stop by the Church Lord and give each of Your Sheppard's a word from a high that will continue to lead Your sheep from going astray, it's just a matter of time that You will rein all by Yourself and Satan will have no more part and Jesus, I just want to be a part of that nation. In Jesus name, I pray. Amen.

Chapter 8

Dear Father,

This morning I peeked from behind my curtain as I watched this administration hand cuff, leg-shackle and chain them around their waist to lead them off to prison. I was so reminded of my first journey twenty-five years ago and the fear that my heart held. I prayed to God that He would be with those first timers to give them strength, guidance and protection. For those that didn't know Him to reveal Himself to them. They were hauled off with only what they had on, not able to take NOTHING with them. If their families didn't come, get their belongings they would be thrown away. Bless them Dear Lord.

For this day I am certain of His Divine Spirit that dwells inside of me. I've been uncomfortable and restless these past few days. I know I'm not going crazy but I've been having lots of uneasy thoughts and to a certain degree hearing voices, someone calling my name so clear whereas I would respond and then I'd feel so strange as chills would cover my body, without doubt, I felt the presence of someone here in the cell with me, but I did refuse to turn over. Like Clare & Mike would say "where's the money", I said; release me, I'm ready to go home. It felt as instant. I fell asleep. I woke up early as usual and I thought about it. Satan has power but not over God. He enters into your mind and cause you or me to this and act upon his deceitful acts of sins, but I dare give him credit for producing Himself in the form of spirt whereas I can feel his presence. I will not give him that much credit. All my life, I've tried staying in touch with my full awareness and presence of the Lord. I may have made some wrong choices in my life and done some things that may not been pleasing to God, yet, by no means am I perfect or the antichrist, but I know that God has His hands on me and that the illumination of His Power are protecting me at all times and that where I am, have been and where I am to go is a part of His Holy and Divine Will upon my life. As I pray Father God, that Your will for me will be done and to guide me in which ever directions that You send me because I know in my right mind I would not go on my own without carrying You in my heart and that my journeys don't be long and that whatever inflictions I may sustain that I can bare because they are "NOTHING" compared to the cross You carried for me and for this I am so forever grateful for all of Your mercy...Forgive me for my trespass as I've forgiven those that has trespassed against me. In Jesus name, Amen.

Thank you Lord. I'm up early preparing my breakfast, just finished with my medications. I wasn't up to writing these past couple of days because I was down and sick. Thank You for answering my prayers. I did get "THAT" letter from Clare, then one from Phyllis and Latrice. Aww you really did show these people up because it's nicer knowing that people do care.

Lord, I pray for those two juveniles back there in that cold room. I ask that Your love and comfort will warm their heart, spirit and feet so that You may guide them. I am too familiar with the journey they are embarking upon and realize the aftermath of their destination. In the name of Jesus I ask that You will turn them around before they get anywhere near as far as I have. I thank You in advance for the wonderful things I know that You will do with their lives.

I thank You for the travel and grace for Clare, Jennifer, Casey Latrice and Leigh Ann for traveling up and down that dangerous highway and Lord Shun Surles to be able to go from city to city. Thank You for keeping that death angel from over my family and friend's families. If I had 10,000 tongues I couldn't tell You thank You enough. In Jesus name, I pray. I ask that You will forgive me for my trespasses as I've forgiven those who as trespassed me. Keep us all at the mercy of Your Throne. Lord keep on watching over my daddy's wife, my brothers, sisters, aunts, uncles and cousins. Keep Aunt Jurleen close to Your heart. Lord, I say Thank You and Amen.

Sunday, January 5, 2014

Heavenly Father,

Thank you, thank you for waking me up this morning. Thank you for my daily bread. Your word, Your confirmation of how much You love me even before I was created in my Mother's womb. You loved me, then you created me. Lord, I thank You for my health, my life, my family and my friends. Father God, I thank You for each of these inmates in here. I am thankful that I am able to learn something from every single person here as I watch, look, listen and love each one. I pray that You bless my tongue with the words of encouragement to uplift these guys that are feeling down and need a word from up high.

Father God, our situations are the same. We're confined in here, in this prison when we could have been in our grave. This prison makes our circumstances the same because You loved us this much to put us together.

Lord, for whatever reason this maybe, I just want to say Thank You for watching over me. I thank you for giving me this moment to draw closer to You, meditate upon Your word and to strengthen our relationship.

Lord, I don't know what tomorrow is going to bring for me, or the day after that, but whatever they bring, I just ask that I be in my right state of mind and focused on You. Bless my family and friends. Bless their health and their finances Lord. Bless the staff members here and teach us to love and respect one another. Father God, show me the way. Teach me how to be obedient and have patience. Bless my ears and heart so that I may listen more closely to Your calling upon me. Lord, whatever my deen is for You, I am more than willing to do. I want more than anything to hear You say "Well done" when my life is over here on this earth. I know at that point I'd be absent from my body and present in Your Heavenly Choir and praising You all the day long. But Father God, right now, I'm just glad to be here and know that You are my Father and I am Your child.

In Jesus name I pray. Amen.

Morning Prayer.

Dear Lord,

Thank You, I just want to say thank You for all You have done for me. I thank You for CoCo's kind words of comfort, concern and confirmation as to where Keith is. Lord, I pray for him because I know that he does not know the significance of Your love and power. Father God, here I am again in the midst of a storm calling upon You to please calm it down as I pass through it. Father, You know that I am not a stranger calling upon You. I call upon You in the midst of my storms and I praise You in my joyous and happy moments. Again, I want to thank You for Tray Turner's confirmation that he's calling upon You. I remember fifteen years ago he was confused and lost in Your word, but You shined Your light upon me for him to see and Lord, I am forever and ever grateful for that. I'm only trusting that You are working in him for him. I thank You or keeping that watchful eye on him in the midst of his storm.

Father God, it's children like him that I am so very grateful for that hear Your word, see Your service and recognize Your blessings. This causes them to believe in You and from there they start feeding the positivity of Your words of encouragement back to us as Your children. Thank You Lord.

Heavenly Father, I know that I'm not in agreement with Bobby, Casey, Clare nor Lisa right now, but I still ask that You will bless them according to their hearts and watch over them. Give them peace that surpasses all their understandings. Show them that it's not about them at no time. Take away any areas of pride in which they don't see in themselves. Take away their selfishness so that their blessing will not be blocked. There is nothing that I need to ask them for, in which You will not provide for me, You always have and for that I am so very grateful.

I ask that You will bless the rest of my family and friends the same.

Lord, please help each inmate and the staff members here in Jesus name I pray. Amen.

Tuesday Night's Prayer

Heavenly Father,

I just want to say thank You, thank You for another day. Thank You for watching over me and keeping me out of harm's way. Lord, thank You for just being You, my Father. You are better to me than I am to myself.

Father God, tonight I was present when this young man confessed that he knew of You and had never given himself to You and accepted You as his Savior. Father God, I know that I don't have the power in here, nor does anyone else in here have the power to bless that young man the way he needs You. Lord, I ask in Jesus name that You will stop by his cell tonight and reveal to him who You are. He's reaching out to You Father God and he was not ashamed to come forth and humble himself without pride. Lord, I am so grateful for You, for Your presence and Your empowering presence. I am reminded Father God, in Your scriptures when You called someone into Your service from Moses stories for examples in Exodus – 3:11-12, Joshua -1:1-9, Gideon – Judges 6:12, and Jeremiah – 1:6-8. Your message was, I can be strong and courageous because You are with me. Victory isn't about my abilities, my strength, my skills, my armor, my gifts or my dedication; it is completely centered on Your presence in me. I can be strong because You will be strong in and through me. Father God, I know that You know how difficult our life is and You are aware of the details of each struggle we will ever face. It tells me this in Your word that we were predestined. You knew us before You created us in our Mother's womb. Lord, I trust and believe in You personally and I know You for myself. Please Father God, do not allow this child to go astray nor have him mislead in Your word. I ask that You will bless not only my tongue, my mind, and my heart but those that are taking a leadership in sharing Your word with others. Be with us, teach us, guide us, and comfort us when we are representing You to others. None of us are in our situation in this prison from being perfect. I have no hidden agendas when sharing Your word, nor Your love, because I am who You made me to be and I am grateful that I am totally different from everyone else in here. Father God, one thing for certain and two for sure Your word is the same 1000 years ago, yesterday, today and right now. Sin is sin, there's no big or small and that if it wasn't for Your grace and mercy, I would not be sitting here talking to You now, and for that – I am so very grateful. Heavenly Father, Thank You.

Dear Heavenly Father,

I thank You for waking me up this morning and in my right state of mind, able to dress myself, feed myself, put on my clothes by myself and most of all have my heart and mind regulated on You.

Lord, I thank You for Your word this morning, when Paul challenged the Colossians "Whatever we do in word or deed, do all in the name of You, Jesus and do it heartily, as to the Lord and not men, knowing that from the Lord we will receive the reward of the inheritance" (Col. 3:17, 23-24). Heavenly Father, I know that You notice and delight in using us. I ask that You will bless my words today with encouragement that will enrich someone's situation or circumstance.

Heavenly Father, on my way to sleep last night, that young man that was reaching out for You, was heavy on my heart. I feel confident that Your sprit from Heaven connected to Your spirit that dwells inside of him and that this morning, that young man is walking in the light and for that I am so very grateful. Let Your light shine upon him so that children like me and him may see our way to the light. Thank You, thank You Father God, for all that You have done for me, in me, and the things that You are doing through me.

Father, I know that in (Romans 10:9) says "That if thou shalt confess with thy mouth the Lord Jesus, and shalt believe in thine heart that God hath raised him from the dead, thou shalt be saved." Let today be a new beginning of life for him, for me, and for all that shall read these words and confess therefore after be saved in Jesus name. Again, Father God, what I want for me, I want for all because I know that You are in the blessing business and have way more than enough to supply us all by the ten folds and Father, in my heart my cup is running over with Your love, your spirit and blessings and for this I am so grateful. Every second of the minute that I have breath is a blessing from You, Your love, grace and mercy. Your spirit continues to live within me and my gifts are blessings…. Thank you, thank you, thank you Lord for being so good to me.

I thank You for my health, I thank You for my family and friends, I thank You for my fiancé, I thank You for each of these inmates that are receptive to my prayers and pray that they encourages them, up-lift them in Your name and sets a foundation for them in how important it is to have a relationship with You whereas, we can pray, talk, cry and laugh but most of all humble ourselves unto You and just say "thank You Lord for dying upon the cross for me." Thank you Our Father, which art in Heaven. Hallowed be thy name. Thy Kingdom come, thy will be done on earth as it is in Heaven. Give us this day or daily bread and forgive us our trespasses as we forgive those who have trespassed against us. Lead us not into temptation, but deliver us all from evil for thine is the Glory, the Power, forever and ever. Amen, Amen, Amen. Thank You Jesus.

Thursday, January 9th, 2014

Heavenly Father,

Thank You Father for waking me up this morning and filling my body with the spirit of life and of your presence. I can feel you all over me this morning. I thank You for waking me up in the wee hours this morning so that I could meditate upon Your word from the visions in my dreams I was having.

Lord, I thank You for my health, my family and friends and Father, I thank You for my finances. You just keep on blessing me.

Heavenly Father, I thank You for watching over me and keeping me out of harm's way. I thank You for the inmates that I am able to communicate with and those that I do fellowship with. Those that have yet to understand me but pass judgment upon me and dare to challenge themselves. I ask that You will shine Your light upon me, bless my words so that they will be Your words of encouragement and scripture that I can share to lift up someone else. I want them to understand Your word and know that we are all one big happy family connected through the blood of Jesus.

Lord, I ask that You will bless all of us, our families and staff here with understanding of Your word so that we will all be on one accord of loving one another and respecting one another so that the peace among us will be of Your presence in our midst.

Father God, I ask that You will bless those that are on the battle fields, in the nursing homes, those of us in jails and prisons, the homeless ones, those that needs You and don't know where to look. Father, You know all of our hearts and our needs. Please supply us with what we need and then bless us according to our deeds, services and hearts.

Father God, bless my heart and mind with the song of lyrics so that I may give extended praises unto You. I thank You for the many gifts and talents that You have given to me. Thank You Lord, in Jesus name I pray. Our Father, which art in Heaven, hallowed be thy name, thy kingdom come. Thy will be don on earth as it is in Heaven. Give us this day, our daily bread and forgive us our trespasses as we forgive those who trespassed against us. Lead us not into temptation but deliver us from evil. For thine is the kingdom, the glory, the power forever and ever. Amen.

Dear Heavenly Father,

Thank You Lord, thank You for waking me up this morning in my right mind. I thank you that I am able to feed myself, clothe myself, and have my heart and mind regulated on You. I just thank You.

Father God, I ask that you will watch over those two young men fighting yesterday. Let that be a lesson to everyone that you just can't go around calling people out of their names, intimidating others because you're in a gang and judging a book by its cover in thinking since you don't belong in a gang you can't fight. Father God, I trust and believe that You will give us the strength we need when we need it. I trust You to watch over me, keep me out of harm's way. In Jesus name, I ask that Your presence will fill this unit, teach us to love one another, respect one another, inmate to inmate and inmate to staff and staff back to inmate, keep us all in accord to Your love and respect.

Thank You for my family and friends Lord. May You bless them and all the inmates here and throughout the entire system. Bless their love ones, our health, give our mind the wisdom to understand and meditate upon Your word. Bless our finances. Bless our tongues so that only words of encouragements will flow from our mouths.

Heavenly Father yesterday a lot of people met with the parole and revocation board and the news was not what they were expecting to hear, but You already knew the outcome. They should have too knowing their situation and the things they have not brought forth to you. Lord, I just thank You for allowing me to serve and worship You in good times and in bad times. When I'm free from jail and prisons and when I am locked up in them, I know to call upon You all the time no matter where I am, what I'm doing, I know that there's no place I am that You won't come and for this I am so very grateful.

I just ask that You'll give me the strength I need to persevere the long run. Use me the way that You see fit as I'm here. I know Father that this is one of Your ways of revealing Yourself through life's tragedies to me. I lost my dad on this journey, some close friends, the hardship that I'm facing daily. But in Your word, You said "You would not put upon me more than I can bear." Lord, I'm holding You to this. I feel that I'm at the lowest in my life and right now, I need You in Jesus name. Our Father, which art in Heaven. Hallowed be thy name. Thy kingdom come, they will be done on earth as it is in Heaven. Give us this day our daily bread and forgive us our trespasses as we forgive those that have trespassed against us. Lead us not into temptation but deliver us from evil. For thine is the kingdom, the glory, the power forever and ever... Amen, amen, amen. Thank You Jesus.

Dear Heavenly Father,

Thank You for Your word this morning. Thank You for waking me up in my right mind and able to pick up my Bible and read Your word. Father God, I ask that you will bless my heart and mind as I give them diligently, add to my faith, virtue and to virtue knowledge so that I may understand Your word as Jesus did. Add to my knowledge temperance, and to temperance patience; and to patience godliness; Father, and to my godliness brotherly kindness, then charity. Keep me on the path of righteousness and don't let me go astray.

Lord, I desire to do right by You. I struggle every second of the minute and every minute of the hour and day by day. Teach me how to be obedient. Give me the strength to stay steadfast and consistent in your word daily and forever how long I need to be in it. Give me the patience to sit humbly and gladly to share Your word with others and a joyful time to sing praises unto You.

Heavenly Father, right now, I am surrounded by men that need Your word and Your blessings just as I do. Comfort us, teach us to love one another and depend upon on another as we are to encourage, uplift and draw strength from each other to manifest the holiness of our spirit to come in accordance of Your will for us as we congregate into Your vineyard and minister, obey and witness the blessings of Your word. I need You and as always I want for my brother the same that I want for me. Salvation is the miracle of a moment; growth is the labor of a lifetime. Father God, at the end of this journey, I want to hear You say "Well done my good and faithful servant" as I move on into eternity with You.

Bless our family, friends, health, our finances, our hearts and minds. Watch over us with Your protective eye and keep us out of harm's way. Bless the staff members of this prison each on according to their hearts. Give them the patience, love, understanding and compassion to treat us with dignity and respect as Your children. Lord, I just want to say thank You, thank You for all that You have done for me and all that You are about to do. I just say, thank You, thank You, thank You.

Our Father, which art in Heaven. Hallowed be thy name. Thy kingdom come, they will be done on earth as it is in Heaven. Give us this day our daily bread and forgive us our trespasses as we forgive those that have trespassed against us. Lead us not into temptation but deliver us from evil. For thine is the kingdom, the glory, the power forever and ever... Amen, amen, amen. Thank You Father in Jesus name Amen.

Dear Heavenly Father,

Thank You for waking me up this morning and my last night laying down. Thank You Lord for watching over me and keeping me out of harm's way. Thank You for the inmates in here that joins together to fellowship and praise Your Holy name and thanks for allowing the pod officers cooperation's.

Father God, Thank You for blessing me with a humble heart, open mind and the gift of love to be able to communicate with my peers. Give us the courage and strength daily to continue our walk together in all the difference services that we contribute to encourage and uplift one another in Your Word Father. I do believe in it takes a village to raise a child. In this prison, as a Christian believer, we are guardians over the youth in Your kingdom and it's our rightful duty to introduce them to Your word. Lord, I am trying to do right by You. I want for my brothers what I want for me and that's to be closer to You and walk in Your light.

Heavenly Father, I ask that You will bless our families, friends, finances, our hearts, bodies with good health and minds with the wisdom to understand then share Your word. Bless our tongues so that our words will be encouraging and uplifting to one another. In Jesus name - Our Father, which art in Heaven. Hallowed be thy name. Thy kingdom come, they will be done on earth as it is in Heaven. Give us this day our daily bread and forgive us our trespasses as we forgive those that have trespassed against us. Lead us not into temptation but deliver us from evil. For thine is the kingdom, the glory, the power forever and ever... Amen, amen, amen. Thank You Jesus.

Night Prayer

Dear God,

Thank You for another day. Thank You for watching over me. Lord, You've been so good to me. I thank You for the life of Martha (Babyhead) Hayes, may her heart and soul rest in peace. I just was talking about her and dreamed of her. Father God, I know that You're showing me things in my dreams and then when I put them together, they are revelations. Lord, right now, I ask that You will comfort Kevin, Larry, Jo Ann and all of her love ones and friends.

Heavenly Father, I want to thank You for my family and friends. I ask that you will bless them in their health, finances, their hearts and minds so that they will be fixed on You. Father God, I ask that You will bless each of us inmates and their families too.

Oh Lord, it's just so hard. I can only imagine what Kevin is going through being the only child and how in spite of all of her short comings to being a mother, she loved him, stood by him, supported his drug addictions and got herself together and Father I commend her and pray that she had straightened her business out with You. I just know her, Johnson, Mott and Eddy Greedy is up there having a time. I thank You for all the good times that we shared together. I sure hat that I am in here. Lord, please give me the strength and release from here. I don't want to be in here anymore when my family and friends are passing on.

I thank You for Clare Lord. I know we don't always see eye to eye on things but we love each other, we try and worship and praise You together. If something should happen to her I just don't think I'd want to go on. Watch over Chris as he is out there in his dangerous line of work. Bless my sister, Jean and give her all the strength she needs to carry on and watching out for her mother. She did all she could do with our dad and I am so very grateful for her. Thank You Lord.

Lord, I've turned Bobby, Casey and Lisa over to You. I do pray that Andriyiah and Emory will not have to inherit that low self-esteem and that Your word will teach them their self-worth and self-value. I pray that You have Your hands on Amber and her children and keep a close eye on Cindy.

I had no control as to choosing my family. You chose me for this family and Lord, I've tried my very best with them all and even when things seem at its worst, I trust and believe that You are working it out for us all.

I'm grateful that Willie James got baptized today. That is so wonderful. I'm so grateful that I'm able to worship with Bubba. I just wish we all could get in one big church together and praise You without a funeral. A family that prays together, stays together. Our Father, which art in Heaven. Hallowed be thy name. Thy kingdom come, they will be done on earth as it is in Heaven. Give us this day our daily bread and forgive us our trespasses as we forgive those that have trespassed against us. Lead us not into temptation but deliver us from evil. For thine is the kingdom, the glory, the power forever and ever. Amen.

Heavenly Father,

Thank You for my last night laying down and waking me up this morning. Father God, I thank You for the Sweet Rest, whereas, I had no tossing or turning in my sleep. I thank You Lord, for waking up able to praise You, read Your word, dress myself and eat my own breakfast, Lord, I just thank You for watching over me, I thank You for the seen and unseen blessings that You have bestowed upon me.

Father God, I'm so grateful to know that before I even ask You for what I think I need, You are already in preparation of blessing me because You know before I ask. I ask right now in the name of Jesus that You will bless my heart, my mind, and my tongue so that the words I speak will be pleasing unto You, encouraging and uplifting to those that I encounter. May Your light shine upon me as a reflection of Jesus so that others may see Your goodness through me.

Heavenly Father, I thank You for my family, my friends that are few, I thank You for these inmates that I am able to share my prayers and Your word with. I thank You for my health and my finances. Father, I thank You in the times of my trials and tribulations because I know that in the midst of them when my poor little heart is broken and mind is full of confusion, I'm able to call upon You and You are here to comfort me, fill my heart and mind with gladness. It is then, that I know You love me so much to comfort me, to take away my worries and give me a peace of mind and for that I am so very grateful.

Lord, You know each of our situations and that our circumstances are different but I know that You are able to handle every single one of us that put out trust in You and Father, bless us according to our faith and our hearts. You already know the outcome to our situation. I ask in the name of Jesus that You will guide us, comfort us, protect us, and walk with us. Teach us how to be obedient to Your word. Give us the strength to withstand our storm. Humble our hearts so that we all can love and respect one another in spite of our indifferences, but because we are all Your children. Take away the judgmental from our sight and fill our hearts with humility so that our service will be to help each other to overcome what's not pleasing to You.

Our Father, which art in Heaven. Hallowed be thy name. Thy kingdom come, they will be done on earth as it is in Heaven. Give us this day our daily bread and forgive us our trespasses as we forgive those that have trespassed against us. Lead us not into temptation but deliver us from evil. For thine is the kingdom, the glory, the power forever and ever... In Jesus name I pray. Amen.

Dear God,

I just want to thank you for my basic needs. Thank You for Your strength, protection and Your empowerment through my sense of belonging, sense of worth, and sense of competence. I am so content in knowing that I don't have to fit in to be accepted because I know that Jesus shows me that I matter by when He went to the cross. I am competent because You has sent Your Holy Spirit to dwell in me that empowers me.

Father God if by chance I am lacking in any of these areas, please strengthen me, pull me back up, because somewhere during my circumstance Satan has stolen my joy and I can't understand Lord, I need You twenty-four-eight, I need You a day in advance, keep me close to You and never let me go astray. Father, I am leaning on You. I am listening to Your word with my heart and seeing beyond my faith for You. I can't do this on my own. I'm struggling every minute of the day Father God and satan is on my trail so I need You more than ever.

Heavenly Father, I know that You have Your hands on me. You have a divine plan for my life beyond this here prison cell and I await it with open arms. I've walked beyond these doors several times and seems to return. Lord, this time send me out on a complete mission for You. Use me in the vineyard of Your Holy Services. I know the position now that You have for me. All I ask is that You give me the strength to keep it consistent as I have for these past thirty days. I thank You for the desire to keep this going this long and to have unspeakable joy doing this. I am so grateful to see how all the guys are coming together and fellowshipping, singing and praising Your Holy name. In Jesus name I pray. Amen.

Chapter 9

Not Knowing How or When to Let Go

Yet, I find myself some twenty something years later of thinking about Travis. How he's doing? What would we be doing today? Would he still be living in Huntsville or San Francisco? He definitely loved to travel and see the world. That's one of many things that we had in common.

I can remember as if it was just yesterday of having the same conversations over again with Travis over twenty years ago. Chris almost ten years ago, Ms. Bamp eight years ago and my Mom five years ago. This worries me now as I think about it. It's about death and what our purpose of being here meant to each other. Bless his heart, I'll always love you, but Travis told me sitting in his apartment after we'd gone to see Patti Labelle in Nashville, that my purpose was to see that his remaining dying days was to see that he was happy and to take care of him. It's strange that all of these people had the same thing in common for my purpose and yet, to this day they never told me what theirs were for, after searching their hearts I found them all to be just as I am with the same purpose because it was a joyful blessing that God granted me the opportunity to be a part of their lives and to know that I was really, really appreciated. During the little time that I was afforded to take care of Travis, we spent so much time talking about the good times we had as children and when we found out we were brothers, he felt just as stupid as I did because we should have been able to look at on another to know that something somewhere had to happen because our genetic genes were too much alike. Our parents never told us about one another until one of our mutual friends told us. We talk about our daddy and his daddy, how they used to come by together and bring us different kinds of food in which they'd gone out and hunted and killed, or had picked from fields and trees. He loved our daddy and it was his love for him that showed me how to love my daddy even more. The days that were better than most, he'd want to help me clean and cook. We'd have some good times in the kitchen. To this day, the fondest memories I have of him is when I am cooking. We would add everything to a meal not stretching it, but adding flavors. We'd mix sweet and hot together for desert, usually bell peppers to everything, it was his love for red onions that has me crazy about them. We would sing and dance as we cleaned and cooked, listening to the blues that WEUP would play on Saturday mornings. It was cold when he first got sick and together, we could not do too many things that involved going outside because he had a very weak immune system. I didn't take chances going around lots of people because I could not afford bringing any cold or flu type symptoms back to him. I cooked a lot of greens, whether they were collards, turnips, or spinach. Some I'd mix. A pot of beans would last almost as long as the greens, sweet potatoes and macaroni and cheese did not tarry long in the house with us. Normally I'd have to open up another box and fry more hot water cornbread at the same time. We rarely had company unless it was Bamp or Chris coming by to pick up plates for themselves, because they didn't feel like cooking, or to stop in to check on Travis and to sit with him while I ran my errands. He really like them and I was so grateful for them.

It was in late January that his mom had decided to move him back to Tennessee. He didn't want to go and I didn't want him to go. I knew I could not go there with him and I knew he wasn't going to like it and low and behold he didn't. After a week or so he ended up in the VA hospital in Murfreesboro where he later died an unhappy death. For all these years I've haunted myself for not being there with him and for him. The same happened with Chris. I was incarcerated at the time that Chris took sick with the same illness as Travis, some twelve years later. I'd always accused them of messing around but they both denied it and carried it to their graves. Ms. Bamp and Chris drove all the way from hot Atlanta to only, Tennessee just to see me because Chris wanted to tell me himself that he was dying from AIDS. I remember sitting in the visitation gallery facing him, all three of us holding hands praying and crying together. We discussed how and when and where, but could never pin point a person or location, but how we knew not using protection. Me not knowing that Ms. Bamp was suffering too. He never made mention of it, even up to the last minute he'd left my house in Tennessee heading back to Atlanta, only to return for his birthday because I was going to cook and invite all our friends up to celebrate. Chris and I use to always go out together. Everyone thought we were brother and sister and it reminded me of hanging out with Travis how I still miss him now.

I can sometimes feel their presence in my midst. There are times like now that I think of them and get this ball of joy inside of my stomach, a chill to roam my body, out the corner of my eye, a shadow to pass, there are so many things to remind me that they are absent from the body and present with the Lord and for that spirit dwells amongst me in the flesh and for this I am so grateful. I guess it don't matter if I learn how to let go or not, they will always be a part of me. I can remember sitting in the room with my mom in 2005 and telling her Bamp died, she became so quiet and still as if she went into a coma. I just sat there and watched her. I could only imagine that she was laying there in praying asking God to please judge his heart and not his soul and let him in. I know the same payer she had for me, she had for him because she loved him as if he was one of her own. After several minutes, she turned to me with tears in her eyes and asked me was I alright. We just sat there and talked for the longest. I always gave her flowers as she lived so we could smell them together. We had some of our best moments in the nursing home. I was there every day, feeding her, combing her hair, watching TV or just taking a nap in the chair. She looked for me, if I was late, she'd call or have the nurse to call. When I moved to Nashville a little over an hour away, I came every other day, then I'd spend longer hours. I'd bring food for the nurses to feed her when she wanted it and pack her drawers with can goods and snacks. She never wanted for nothing. I knew my purpose was as with Travis to make her as content and happy as possible. I just wish that Ms. Bamp would have told me that she was sick as she was. To this day, I just say it was her high blood pressure, because that's what she told me before going into her coma, but rumor has it that she died of AIDS. Regardless if its AIDS, cancer, diabetes, murder, heart attack, stroke, or hit by a car, train, and even falling out of the sky in an air plane, when that time comes, it's according to the Divine Will of God's plan that He foreseen our death, the date, time, year and cause with our births and if anyone believes different is shame on them, but one thing is for sure and two for certain, we will all cross that river of death regardless of our cause. I just pray that your hearts will be as genuine as I knew Travis, Chris, Bamp and Lucy Mae's were. I think of Dee, Ms. Frankie, Sheila and Crystal Blue. Ms. Baba, Brewser, Mayberry there are so many others that I knew were good to me as I was to them that are amongst God's Angels that are watching over me and someday I'll be joining them to watch over you, all that I so dearly love. Having to say good-bye has been, is and will always be hard for me. Letting go so as I get older, my memory may fade but the scars of their love will be forever carved around my heart.

From this day forward to the rest of my days left here in this old world, on my birthday I will lay flowers and send balloons with their names on them up in the air as a token of my love and the joy they brought to my life. April 21, will forever be their day to.

Chapter 10

I Was Not Built to Break

- God has planted eternity in the human heart. Ecclesiastes 3-11
- Abraham Lincoln once said "Surely God would not have created such a being as man to exist only for a day! No, no, man was made for immortality."
- We never see things the way they are, we see them the way we are. God said (Isaiah 44-2) I am your Creator; you were in my care even before you were born."
- The Bible says "God will fulfill His purpose for me" (Job 12-9-17)
- Life on this earth is a test. God continually tests people's character, faith, obedience, love, integrity and loyalty. Words like trials, temptations, refining and testing occurs more than 200 times in the Bible. God tested Jacob when he had to work extra years to ern Rachel as his wife. Adam & Eve

failed their test in the Garden of Eden and David failed his test from God on several occasions. But the Bible also gives us many examples of people who passed a great test, look at Joseph, at Ruth, Ester and Daniel. Character is both developed and revealed by tests. We are always being tested. I know that God have, is and always watches my response to people, problems, success, conflicts, illness, disappointment and how I react to the weather. He even watches the simplest things such as picking up a piece of trash, how you treat and respect homeless people to a waitress in a restaurant. I remember when my mom died. I closed her eyes for her, watched her take her last breath and thought about how God gave me the first breath through her and a few hours later how she watched my eyes open. A few months after her death, I was later diagnosed with all the sickness she had. I didn't complain because I knew that God was testing me. I'd took good care of my

Mother and God knew that I could handle this better than my brother or sisters. The times I went to prison was to test my bitterness, each time I embraced my journey as a mission to help others to sing praises unto Him and to show others how easy it is to build a relationship with God personally. I don't yet know my full purpose of Gods will for my life, but according to His two commandments when He came back was to "Love God with all we have and to love our neighbors as we love ourselves" and I've tried my best with all I know to, to honor those two commandments. I don't hate people, for those that has trespassed against me, I pray for. I treat them nice. By way of me doing anybody wrong, I pray and ask God for forgiveness. Everything I've ever done wrong, I did it to myself. I don't think I can carry the cross and burden on my back of hurting others. God has blessed me with lots of money and I know again, it was a test to see how I'd react to the greater riches He has in store for me. I gave more of it away than I used helping others. Do I have regrets – well no, because if I died, I could not carry it with me, and it would have only left problems for Clare to leave it just for her and none for the rest of my family. I can to pass them. People judge me from the outside, but they don't see my heart nor do they know my relationship with God. I'm not trying to impress anyone, not even God. I just live and treat people the way I want to be treated but in the process give God all of my praises. For this I am so very grateful......

Chapter 11

Good morning world.

Thank you Jesus for waking me up this morning and I'm able to use my every limb. I've taken my medicine for diabetes, high blood pressure, high cholesterol and a pain pill. I thank you for my medicines to keep me going....so I won't complain...

Lord, I thank you for court yesterday and the blessings that You bestowed upon all of us. I prayed and asked that you would take care of it and Father, you did it in a way that you blessed all ten of us. I thank you for them that knew not of your blessing, thank you Lord.

You know I wasn't able to reach Clare yesterday when I came in from court, but Lord I know she was probably at Bible Study; and I Thank you for her Lord.

I am on my way to have my blood sugar checked and return for breakfast. I really hate that I'll then be a prey for all these perverts. I am really missing Reuben. I'm missing Marcel and I just hope that he is okay and that I'll go back to his cell. I really like being in the cell with him.

Today, I do not want a celly. My celly just left and I was not able to write, but today and this weekend this is all I want to do.

Here I sit in my cell all confused. I've endured so much heart ache and pain in these few hours of the day. I thank you Lord and I won't complain. I went to the law library to obtain documents that I thought would help my legal situation, but that was a dead end. I know Satan is busy but God has His best interest for me. I dare to sit at this grave any longer for I've given it to God.

I went to sick call and what I went for was not my problem. I was fine until I took my right shoe off and saw my foot. All kinds of flags went up. I had to be treated for this. Samples had to be sent to the lab because I have a fungus growing inside my toes that are very serious to my diabetes and could possibly have to have my foot cut off. I am really tired now.

Upon returning to the unit, I see my baby and we're both excited to see one another even though we both have received some very bad and upsetting news. He goes first and boy was this a hard pill to swallow. He has a murder charge and he promised to me on his two precious kids that he did not do the killing and that there is no evidence nor witness to say he did it, but the district attorney has come up with this convincing theory to present to the jury...I said to run it. However, it's easy from my point of view to say this, but its logical...for one, he'll have everything on record for an appeal. Two, he could get an intellectual jury that knows about the law and trials and that if there's no physical evidence there's no case. But the DA knows he did not commit this murder, but wants him to admit to another one, therefore they can stick it to him for both murders. The system tries to be slick, but the defense attorney is ineffective, because he seems to be biting on the DA side. But in the mean time I am doing all I can to help him. I didn't even bother to tell him about my little mess. I am not looking at nowhere near as much time as he is. The most I could get is 8 years and I'm not going for that. As to my medical, I am just going to hold up about it too. I do not want to cause anymore sadness to him and the sad part is that I know him from the news. I saw this case on TV.

I don't understand how and why I am getting close to these guys with all this time like I am going to be here with them. Starting right now, I have decided that I am free and I'm going home in November so that I will not be involved with anyone else with more time than I have. That way I will not end up like "prom star" dead.

My friend Pony is cool. We have had a pretty good day so far.

1 Chronicles 16:34 "Oh, give thanks to the Lord, for He is good? For His Mercy endures forever."

Dear God,

Thank You so much for waking me up this morning and for my last night laying down. I thank You for being in my right mind able to dress myself get up to go take my insulin and to be able to feed myself, but most of all to have my heart and mind focused and sat on You.

Lord, I thank You for me not having to worry about what I eat, drink, have to put on or even about tomorrow. I praise You and I thank You for all You have done, doing right now and will do.

Father God, I trust You upon Your word and my testimony is that my faith in You has not failed because You have always come through for me, even when I continued to sin, Your mercy has favored me and I am so grateful. I am grateful for the understanding of this saying "worry does not empty tomorrow of its sorrows, it empties today of its strength." In James 3-17:18 sums it up.

But the wisdom that is from above is first pure, then peaceable, gentle, and easy to be treated, full of mercy and good fruits, without partiality, and without hypocrisy. And the fruit of righteousness is sown in peace and them that make peace." Father, I know that to worry is to doubt and question my faith and I am again so humbly grateful that the sincerity and intimate relationship that I have with You secures all my doubts and Father God, I thank You for being God all by Yourself.

Heavenly Father, I thank You for my health, I thank You for my family, my friends and my finances. Lord, I thank You for this storm in my life that I am going through because I know that You have not made a mistake as to where I am supposed to be and what I am supposed to be doing right now in this minute. I ask that You will continue to give me strength each day to survive the attack of Satan and to keep him away from me...I cannot do this all by myself. I need You

Lord. I ask that You will bless each and every inmate here and the staff too Father. Bless each of our family members. Keep us and them out of harm's way. I just want to thank You again Father God.

"Our Father which art in Heaven. Hallowed be thy name, they kingdom come, thy will be done on earth as it is done in heaven; give us this day our daily bread and forgive us our trespasses as we forgive those that have trespassed against us. Lead us not into temptation but deliver us from evil. For thine is the kingdom, the glory and the power forever and ever. Amen. Thank You Jesus."

Heavenly Father,

I want to thank You for Your grace and mercy and Your travelling grace from one end of this state to the other. Thank You Lord. Father, I forgive those young men that showed out so ugly and kept me from going into that gang infested unit. I know it was Your protection that kept me from going in that environment. I ask that You will show them a revelation of what they missed by me not coming in and that when they shall need me, I will be humble to help them in Jesus name.

Father God, I trust that this was Your plan for me to come here because I sure didn't want to come here. Now that I am here, I just ask that You will watch over me and keep me out of harm's way. Use me as You desire for me to spread Your word.

Lord, I ask that You will allow me to come in contact with one of these counselors that will be able to assist me in getting my time situated and that the court will give me the time that is owed to me by Giles County and then Lord that this confusion in Davidson Count to be resolved and over with Father God, that then after all of that is over and done with You will take control over my life so that I may be able to live a free, productive, and good life where my services in Your vineyard will be appreciated, accepted and enjoyed.

I thank You for my family and friends. I thank You for the inmates that are nice to me and those that are not also. I just pray that You will bless me with your light upon me so that the insecurities they have of themselves, You will fulfill them with the love, self-worth, strength, caring, understanding, self-value, respect for others and themselves, the Holy Spirt and the humility to see people as they want people to see them, to accept them, understand them and treat them with the respect they deserve as being Your children.

Our Father which art in Heaven. Hallowed be thy name, they kingdom come, thy will be done on earth as it is done in heaven; give us this day our daily bread and forgive us our trespasses as we forgive those that have trespassed against us. Lead us not into temptation but deliver us from evil. For thine is the kingdom, the glory and the power forever and ever. Amen. In Jesus name. Thank You.

Heavenly Father,

I thank You for waking me up this morning. Lord, I am certain that my purpose is directed and appointed by You. I am grateful to have been placed here before a longtime friend, Grady Brown. Father God, You know that many prayers, the thoughts, the concerns I've talked with You about of him, the sympathy when is mother and sister died, the way his brother has done him...I just thank You for this privilege to make it here to him. Whatever Your divine plan is for me here, please make him apart of it so that I may be able to help him go home.

Heavenly Father, I thank You for my family and friends. I thank You for watching over all of us. I thank You for every inmate in this prison because this is now the family You have chosen for me. I see the good in them because You made all of us. I know that Your Spirit are in all of us and my prayer is that we all connect and come together for the good of one another. Father God, I ask that You will bless each staff member her one by one. Give them the strength and the courage to love us all and respect us. Lord, allow them to be willing to help us in every area that we need them.

Father God, I ask that you will humble these gang members, take the hatred, disrespect and violence away from them so that they may treat these women like queens and not those disrespectful words they call them and treat them. If this were their mother, sister or grandmother and aunt they would be mad. Not to mention their girlfriends or wives. Bless the men and keep them out of harm's way as they are trying to protect us.

Heavenly Father, bless all the guys that came here with me. I know that Gordon isn't happy in his unit, comfort him Father; do it for Coffee too. Lord, rumor has it that Gordon and Bailey will be shipped to another prison when they leave here. My prayer is that when and if they shall go, let them go to the same prison and if possible, become cell mates as they both have a few years to serve. Bless Martin, Gavin, Huddleston, Parham so that they will not get into any trouble here. Lord, Shamus is ready to go home, let him make parole in May and have a good job lined up for him so that he won't have to come back here. Bless Percy Baker and Charles Murphy when they go to court so that they won't get any more time. In Jesus name I pray. Amen.

Heavenly Father,

Thank You Lord, thank You for first loving me. Thank You for picking me back up every time. I've stumbled and felled down. What a blessing that Jesus promises to take my stumbling, disheveled life and present me faultless to You.

Father God, I ask that by and through Jesus that I be cleansed up so that I may be presentable for Your presence. I've lived this here old life of crime and I haven't been selfish with it because I know that it's nothing that I have done that I can say I did on my own whether it was bad or good, You are and always has been the head of my life. I have never been in control of it, even if I thought I was, I was only fooling myself.

Thank You Lord for me being able to look in the mirror and see me for who I am and not what I am because I know that You dwells inside of me and when I see beyond my sight with faith I am able to see Your reflection and Father God, I am so very grateful. I thank You for my family, friends, finances, my health; Lord I thank You for all these new friends that I've met here and I ask that You will bless my tongue so that the words I speak be pleasing to You. I pray that they will be encouraging and uplifting to the ones that read my prayers. Father God, whatever they may be going through in the midst of their storms. I just ask that You will comfort them. I ask that You will protect us and keep us out of harm's way. For those that has been suffering during their storms, I ask that You will let Your light shine upon them.

Heavenly Father, You know my heart and my intentions way better than I do. You know how much I need You and that I can't do anything without You. I don't have the power to bless nothing with these hands of mines, but Father God, I ask that You will bless each and everyone in this prison and the staff members too according to our hearts. In Jesus name Amen. Thank You Lord.

Heavenly Father,

Thank You, thank You for another wonderful and blessed day. I thank You for Jesus; for Him carrying the cross for my sins way before I was born and for me not having to be guilty. Thank You Father, for having me as Your child.

Father God, I know that it's nothing that I have done to be so deserving of Your love, favor and mercy, but by Your grace I am so grateful that You see fit to keep on blessing me. Every day that I wake up is truly a blessing for me. I am grateful to know that You have kept that death angel away from my cell and my family and friends. Thank You God for watching over all of us. I thank You for the guys in this unit and in this program. Father God, You know that I have to have this program and I ask that You will see that

I stay in here and complete it as soon as possible. I already know that it was Your favor up on me to come right on in here. You knew what Your divine plane was for me before I got here and I am so very grateful Father.

Lord, I ask that You will bless all of us in here, our family and friends, our staff members, our health and finances. Give us our daily bread, strength and to watch over all of us, keep us out of harm's way Father.

Heavenly Father, I pray for those that are homeless, at war defending us, in the nursing homes, other prisons, those that are grieving and weeping over their love one. I pray for those that are seeking You and have no guidance light to see through others to find you. I pray for those children that are being abused and neglected. Father God, make Your presence known to those of us that are in these situations and make our circumstances more bearable to live with. Bless our minds and tongues so that our words and thoughts will be pleasing unto You, encouraging and uplifting to one to another, so that we can all work towards that commandment of loving our neighbor as we love ourselves... in Jesus name.

"Our Father which art in Heaven. Hallowed be thy name, they kingdom come, thy will be done on earth as it is done in heaven; give us this day our daily bread and forgive us our trespasses as we forgive those that have trespassed against us. Lead us not into temptation but deliver us from evil. For thine is the kingdom, the glory and the power forever and ever. Amen. Thank You Jesus. Thank You.

Heavenly Father,

I want to thank You for men such as Martin Luther King, Jr., men who walked by faith, making changes in history for our future generations still to come and give You all the glory as he was in full motion. Thank You Father God, that through him, You shined Your light upon for the world to see. Thank You.

Heavenly Father,

I thank You for my last night laying down and my getting up this morning in my right mind, being able to dress myself, go get my insulin shot and feed myself...Thank You Lord.

Father, I don't know what You have in store for me today, but I do ask that You will bless my tongue so that the words I say will be encouraging, uplifting and godly to my peers. May my presence reflect the light of the way so that those are in the dark from You may see Your light through me...use me Father God, for I am worthy.

Bless each of us in this prison, inmates, staff, our families, our friends, finances, health and strengthen us in Your word so that we may be more understanding, receptive, caring and wise children of Yours and be able to lead by examples and walk by faith as Jesus did...giving, You all the glory. Teach us to love, respect and understand one another. Keep us out of harm's way and from under the attack of Satan. Keep us out of the line of being judged by others and persecuted as if they are You and are sin free.

Lord, I thank You for our intimate and personal relationship. I thank You for teaching me, guiding me and showing me how to love one to another. I am grateful for Your divine wisdom that teaches me to love and not be judgmental because we are all

Your children and You are the Father and judge.

I am who I am and not what I am when I am seen by Your eyes. I am Your child and I am so very grateful. I know that I am a sinner saved by Your grace and Father God I thank You. My sin is sin. I thank You. My sin is not larger or smaller than any other sin; sin is sin. I thank You that I've never taken something that was never mine and I could not give back and my prayer to those that have will seek You for their forgiveness, leave it at Your feet and move forward, work diligently in Your vineyard, and be fruitful of Your word, in hope that they may lead and encourage someone back to life that was (is) traveling down the death road...in Jesus name, in Jesus mane I pray. Thank You Lord.

Heavenly Father,

I thank You for Your word this morning and I thank You for just loving me enough to wake me up…Thank You.

Father God, I ask that today each of us inmates in here will use our stewardship in loving one another as we love You and ourselves. That You will bless each of our tongues so that our words will be encouraging and uplifting to one another. Father, allow us to focus on You as we are focusing on going home. If we could just put You first in all we do, everything we do will be in alignment with Your divine will and purpose while we are all here on earth together. I am certain that we are in here at this time because of Your divine purpose. Now, we just have to figure out what that is. On the meantime Lord, I ask that You will watch over us, comfort us during the storms of our lives; bless the staff members here so that we can respect one another and still know our place as inmates without further hardship placed upon us.

Heavenly Father, teach us how to listen with our hearts, show us how to see with our faith. Instill in us the patience to wait upon You without trying to move You when we want to, causing us to miss the beauty of Your blessings.

Lord, I thank You for all of these guys in here. I thank You for the staff members that are here. I thank You for those that take leadership and is not afraid to share Your word.

Father God, I have a special prayer going up for Juan Howell, Betty, Metrice, Amber, Cindy, Shun, Susan and all the others. Betty Lipton was in my dreams this morning. I can't understand them all yet, but the history of them has been visions to prepare me as they did with my father that broke my heart. I just thank You for having him all those years. I know that one day soon I'll see him, my mother, Bam, Travis, Sheila and Whitney Houston too. I just thank You for them.

Our Father which art in Heaven. Hallowed be thy name, they kingdom come, thy will be done on earth as it is done in heaven; give us this day our daily bread and forgive us our trespasses as we forgive those that have trespassed against us. Lead us not into temptation but deliver us from evil. For thine is the kingdom, the glory and the power forever and ever. Amen. Thank You Jesus.

Heavenly Father,

I just want to thank You for waking me up this morning in my right state of mind, being able to dress myself, take my insulin, feed myself and most of all to study Your word with my heart and mind fixed on You.

Father God, as I go into this day, I ask that You will start off blessing my mind with divine wisdom so that I may speak the words of encouragements that will uplift someone who is feeling discouraged and alone in hope that they will discover the beauty in You.

Lord, I am so very grateful to be able to call upon You during the happy and sad moments of my life, the good with the bad, the sunny with the clouds. I am just blessed and You keeps on blessing me.

Heavenly Father, I thank You for watching over me, my family, friends, my children (CoCo, Rod D, C Rick, Jermaine & Nickolas) Lord, whatever they may be going through, I ask that You will be there in the midst of their trials. Ease their burdens Father God. I know that You know each one of their struggles. Show them your light, teach them how to listen for You with their hearts and see You through their faith.

Father, I ask that You will bless each of us here in this unit including our staff team. Bless our families and keep us together. Watch over us. Guide us so that we won't stray away from You. Those of us that need this program, Lord give us the strength to withstand this so that we may go home, back out into the world and work as Your servants. Help us to deliver Your word and let our testimonies in hope keep other children from committing any crimes and coming in here. Use us as Your vessel in Jesus name.

"Our Father which art in Heaven. Hallowed be thy name, they kingdom come, thy will be done on earth as it is done in heaven; give us this day our daily bread and forgive us our trespasses as we forgive those that have trespassed against us. Lead us not into temptation but deliver us from evil. For thine is the kingdom, the glory and the power forever and ever. Amen. Thank You Jesus. Thank You.

Heavenly Father,

Thank You for waking me up this morning. Here it is not even 5:00 a.m. Lord and all I can do is say thank You. I thank You for allowing me to go out get breakfast, take my insulin, come in and get confirmation of Your love for me through Your word.

Over the week-end Father, I was struggling with how You love me and allow all this to happen to me. Now I understand, just as Apostle Paul described his grueling ordeals. He had in his mind a far more exceeding and eternal...glory 2 – Con. 4:17.

Father God, in spite of my situation and circumstance You know in my heart that I love You will all of my might and that there is no second guessing. Yeah, I get upset sometimes, and it's not because things aren't going my way – but because it's so obvious that it's a direct attack on me from satan through authority figures. They are supposed to be Christ like people and it catches me off guard because it feels like You don't be having my back then, but it doesn't stop my love for You.

Heavenly Father,

I thank You for all that You have done for me and I thank You in advance for all that You are about to do for me in my life. You know what I need and my heart's desire. Right now Father, I thank You for keeping that demon of sickness away from my body, that Angel of Death away from my cell and most of all loving me first. Thank You Lord – In Jesus name I pray. Amen.

Chapter 12
In My Last Days

I just want to be happy, serve the Lord, love my neighbors as I love myself, eat healthier and avoid alcohol and drugs. It's gonna be hard for me to do because marijuana should not even be considered a drug. It's a herb that relaxes my aching body from pain, but it makes me feel a certain way – beautiful romantic, sexy, open minded, sometimes very talkative and then HUNGRY.

I'm 51 years old...I've lived my life and for these past 11 years I've been on the run for Jesus. I've had some good days and some bad ones. Lot of hills to climb but when you are doing things for Jesus...Satan will test you and will attack you. Buckle up, fast, and keep your faith. Prayer changes things. When you are able to talk with God, He will reveal Himself to you. See, we fail when we go to trying to look for God with the human eyes, Now Shugga, we have to search, look and listen with our hearts, that's what God judges us by, therefore, no other man can judge us, they can't see within us. Don't believe the hype when they say they do, no prophet nor Muhammad could do that and not even Buddah…but the Spirit of the Lord that dwells within our heart and mind is all that POWERFUL and that POWER is JESUS.

I say these are my last days, but my best days are ahead of me. I know that absent from the body is to be present with Lord. Don't cry for me and let me smell my flowers now.

If there were any regrets that I may have is not getting to know my family. I will not name them out but I just want to say this to the new and upcoming generation: practice what you preach. Don't go out there trying to save the world when your battle field is in turmoil, in other words try a minister to your family. A family that prays together stays together. It just makes you look bad and you have got to have thought about what God would say.

I have brothers & sisters that are so CALLED ministers that honestly believe they have never done any wrong and will look beyond their sins to look down on mines- my life that I live. I have one sister I love so dearly and she knows it. My sister Jean Davis as many grew to love, but growing up everybody used to say I looked just like her. She was my idol and still is. You talking about can sang-that girl can sang. She changed the 'I' to an 'a' in sang. We will go so far in between and the next thing you know we on the phone talking and not missing a beat. I still often wonder how my life would have turned out had my mother let me go with her when she came for me in 1979 – always, I will always love you in my Whitney Houston voice.

Casey, Andryiah, Emory & Amber I could never tell you all how much I love you and appreciate how you all dedicated your free time to the sale of my books.

I didn't live a perfect life but none of my fellow comrades didn't either, but I lived to love and respect for those that stepped on my feet. I pushed you off and you knew not to repeat it.

I just want the family to come together and be happy of one another and supportive. Not just my family but every family. This is the dying wish of every person, just unfortunately, I'm going to live forever – FAME.

I've endured so much in time of the period of my life. I'm not bitter, never have been. I've never asked the universe for much. I've been a go getter with limitations. I'd sacrifice the risk of selling drugs over stealing and robbing, not that one was better than the other. I've always thought that selling drugs was a job verses stealing from someone – I know it's an awful feeling to go for your stuff and it's not there. You keep looking like it's magic and going to pop back up, but it doesn't – that's an awful feeling and knowing that someone has stolen it. All kinds of thoughts go through your mind; you even want to kill them...at that moment.

Robbing is even worse. I'll never forget Super bowl Sunday 2014. I was robbed at gun point over in the projects in South Nashville. The fear has to be the worse that I ever experienced in my life. I could not get over it until I went back to get them Yeah...it happened. They did not kill me or shoot me, but they might as well should have, for several weeks I lived in fear. It was nothing I could do until I went back and show two of the three that robbed me. I had to in Jesus name because I was not to continue to live like that. I don't know but I'm just saying it felt so right. I've run into those guys several times. One in a wheelchair and they have apologized for what they did to me and I explained the effect it had on me and we have moved on.

Selling drugs then was like a job. The system had continued to fail me and I could not get a job, but I had to live. I never held a gun to anyone and made anyone buy my drugs.

Looking back on my past – I always wanted to do right. I just wasn't given the fair chance.

Unless you have actually gone through a molestation and rape as a child you will never know the mental state you endure. As a boy and growing up not liking sex with a girl or ever experiencing it on your own – then at the age of 51 even looking back wondering if it had not of happened would I be a man of a man and not a woman trapped in a man's body. All kinds of things that I could have fault myself for but nowhere near as how society had blamed me for.

By no means was I to turn out serving twenty-six years of my life in prison and on parole for selling not even an ounce of cocaine and not to mention at that time I was on drugs having to cope with my life and what was going on all around me.

Yet, I am still not bitter – Disappointed...Yes. Somehow, I still want to believe that God used this method to keep me preserved. I look back on my days of just having all these men sexually, lost three of my best friends to AIDS and right when I should have been right there with them, but some twelve years later I'm threatened with cancer... The devil is a liar. Here comes its cure because I'm going to kick its ass. Cancer is not ready for my body. Mind over matter will defeat this. I am in control over this.

Just when I thought everything was going good in my life. I had taken my house back, living the good single life, traveling and very supportive in my Church. My sister just graduated college on Saturday with her Masters. My baby sister is almost ready to graduate too. She graduates in April of 2018.

Things just couldn't be better for me. Finally, my son is back home with me, working the best job he has ever had with great pay and benefits.

When I say that God has been extremely GOOD to me. If He never does another thing for me – He has already done enough…

I just really WANTED to believe this.

I woke up graduation morning calling Casey – I was so sick. Real sick. Diarrhea and vomiting. I knew I had to get ready and leave. That was the longest graduation and dinner under my circumstances of not wanting to tell anyone other than Casey that I was sick. When the opportunity presented me with a way out, I literally flew, lol.

Forty-five minutes from home took two hours it seemed like when I got there. I went straight to bed. Up all morning, head hurting like hell. My biggest fear of that was remembering that this awful head ache I was having is what lead to my brother being diagnosed with AIDS. I was in panic mode. I could not take it. I forced myself to get in the shower. My momma always said "make sure you take a bath and put on clean underwear when going to the hospital. I did. I was even able to drive myself to the hospital.

After six long hours, I was hit with some very tragic health issues — I couldn't imagine anything worse — I guess, but it felt like my world had just ended and I have just begun to live to die. I was scared to death. I was there alone, went home alone and I just didn't know what to do or say. I didn't want to tell anyone because I didn't want to worry anyone and I sure didn't want people flocking to me because I'm dying.

I just feel that I have to complete my work here before He calls me home. I remember when I was twelve and got sent away – this is how I felt. I could cling on to anyone but God then. Thank God my granny use to put me on that Joy Bus of Church of Christ growing up. So I knew who God was. The good part now is that I know Him better.

I am not perfect in my deen, but I do strive to do better all the time. He knows my heart and I go overboard to treat people and love them as I do myself and I love God whole heartily. These two things I do all day daily, I am a true tither. When you know that you have done all you can do for the world and when faced with a deathly crisis such as mines...you just give that back to Satan and wait on the Lord to either heal you or call you on home to Glory where my mother, father, my brother, sister and best friends will be there waiting on me with Annie, Jimmy and Willie. I know Ms. Bamp is going to meet me half way to make sure I won't mess up anything. My Angel that has watched over me since 2005. Rest on Shugga, I'll see you soon.

I'm on my way to Los Angeles. This is the only thing that seems to soothe me when I am going through something. I remember in the beginning of 2012 when my dearest John would give me money just to go out there to shop for a couple of days, get my hair and nails done. Just treating me super good, now he will be sending Mike G out here tomorrow to comfort me and be at my bedside. Sometimes we just have to do what we feel – even if it means leaving the ones behind that you love.

I think the most hurting part of this was I never got a phone call from my so call friends to just ask me how I was feeling. Fulvia felt me being sick because I missed her birthday party. Carolyn, she read it on Facebook, then immediately called and ready to come over. It's just I know if it would have been one of my six I would have gotten there. I have bigger things to worry about now.

Satan will test you, but God will take care of you. I'm on His side, even when times are hard. I can hear Jennifer Holiday sing that song in my mind right now as I continue to write.

Even though I have some new friends & family from my Church and school, He still keeps me safe in His arms.

Yeah...I was stressing at first but there's nothing I can do but allow God to do what He is about to do and wait.

For one thing for sure and two things for certain, it ain't over until God say so – Satan ain't got nothing to do with my expiration date. God seen the ending with my beginning and for that I am so very grateful. That means what He has for me is for me...Hallelujah.

I do believe in miracles. I honestly do believe that God is not finished with me yet.

I may not be around to see this miracle here on earth but I will see Him face to face when I walk around Heaven all day long where I will not be crying in pain, faced with the fear of death no more Tennessee lottery, because I will have won something much greater.

As I come to the end of this chapter, I want to leave this to all my readers and loyal fans – Sheila Connors keep me alive – lol.

John 3:16 – That God so loved the world that He gave His only begotten Son so that we may have eternal life and it abundantly.

My life has been extremely abundantly in spite of all that I endured from a child to right now. I look back on all the joy, laughter, the good times that I had with complete strangers across this land. I have never feared going anywhere because I knew God would never lead me anywhere that He would not bring me from.

I don't care what the occasion was, I did tell someone about Jesus.

I want to encourage you all to do the same. Let's make this world a better place. Eat and feed one another – not just on holidays. Visit the sick and shut in. Things you may be tired of, take to the nursing home and put it on them, hang a picture on the wall, share a bouquet of flowers of 7 or 8 dollars with about 10 to 12 people and watch the smile it puts on their faces. Encourage our young boys and girls to strive for their dreams and education. Teach them how to love with respect unconditionally and without bias intentions. My signature "One Love" is just that One Love, One God, one you to fulfill this. God is of many attributes but only one God and shares Himself with the entire WORLD. Just do your part in your community and it will make a big difference.

Chapter 13
My Love Letter to God

My Dearest Love,

As I sit here on my cross journey from Los Angeles to Kansas City by the way of Amtrak. I am reminded of You by the most beautiful sites of Your nature, from the desert, to the valleys, the shapes of Your mountains, the beautiful wild flowers to the cows, horses, rams and birds.

To know that You gave Your only begotten Son so that may have life abundantly here on earth. You loved me first. How can I not love You? Many say they don't see You. I see You in everything that's beautiful. I feel You emotionally through all my challenges. I feel Your comfort through my sorrows. I feel Your joy through my excitement. I know You said You would never leave nor forsake me, so I trust You being with me-that's why I fear nothing but you and that fear is of You leaving me.

When you took my grandmother in 2001, my brother 1991, my sister 1992, best friend Chris 2004, Bamp 2005, Mother 2008, Auntie 2014, Uncles 2016 and Daddy 2013. You just kept showing me how much You loved me to keep me here and for this I am so grateful.

You've given me so much to look forward to as I lay down to go to sleep and to wake up the next morning...I look to You and right now I want to say Thank You and I love you.

Chapter 14
Death

This is something that we all must do – is die.

God seen the ending with the beginning. I am not afraid of dying. I have no control over this.

What I am afraid of is living. We can live the wrong way here on earth and have eternal death here after, which is worse than dying here on earth.

Stephanie Michelle Massey.

Dear God,

Good morning, I love You and I thank You for waking me up this morning and starting me on my way. I thank You again for my last night laying down.

Father, thank You for the confirmation of Your love for me again through Your word. I am so very grateful that you know my heart. Father God, if there's any faults in there please forgive me because they are not my intentions. Yes, Father, I had condemned myself far worse than I once deserved, but thanks for Your forgiveness that I was able to forgive myself. I forgive those that trespassed against me and Lord I ask for forgiveness that I trespassed against. Lord, I strive daily to treat people the way I want to be treated. I ask that Lord, as long as You keep me here, give me the strength, the wisdom and love to keep in going through this journey. First, loving You whole-hearted with all my might and then loving my neighbors as I love myself.

Heavenly Father, I ask that You will bless each of us here in this prison, including the staff that works here through-out this prison. Bless all of our families and friends.

Teach us, guide us and keep us out of harm's way.

Lord, you know our situations better than we do. Some of us don't know how to handle our situations and we are powerless without You. Only a fool can think that he has control over himself. I thank You for being the head and not the tail of my being. Father, I'm so very grateful that You are the lender and not the borrower and most of all, I am so blessed by You in knowing that You Are God, and God all by Yourself. I am so grateful to serve You... thank You, thank You, thank You Lord. I thank You for my health, I thank You for my finances, I thank You for my family and my friends. Lord, I thank You for my trial and my tribulations because I trust and believe that You would never take me anywhere that You could not bring me out of. Lord, I just thank You. I thank You for all the things that You have done for me. I can say "they were all for the good of me, whether it was for someone else." I got the message and I am so very grateful Lord, just keep me continually praising You. In Jesus name… Amen. Thank You Jesus, Thank You.

Heavenly Father,

Thank You Father for waking me up this morning. I thank You for Your watchful eyes over me as I slept. I am so very grateful for the sweet dreams that I had of the Church, the choir, my sister Clare, Lord, I just thank You for all that You have done for me. The more I read in Your word, the more confirmation I get that You are the God of Your word and that all I am doing is in accordance with the will that You have for my life and for this I am so very grateful.

Father God, I want to thank You for all the unseen blessings that You have bestowed upon my life. I thank You for each and every person that has come in and out of my life. Their purpose in my life, I hold dear even if it is a lesson learned out of hardship. For what I do know, that whatever lies ahead of me – You have my back. I know You encourage me more and more to continue my trust in You in all I do not know. You are all I have and that there is no other help I know – I can't look to man for what I know that only You can do and trust that it will be okay. NO!!!

Heavenly Father I need You. My life has no meaning without You. Father guide me, teach me thy way. Show me the way Lord, let my light shine as an example of good to mankind; Help them to see the pattern of Thee, shining in beauty, lived out in me.

Lord you know that I've never professed of being perfect, but Father my heart is pure as gold. I have the right intent. I love You with all my might and I treat and love my neighbors as I want to be treated and loved. I know my daily struggle on this journey and each day that struggle is fading for desire – I know that trickery of Satan can't win. All that He attempts to destroy in my life has no comparison to how You can restore it...

Our Father which art in Heaven, hallowed be thy name, thy kingdom come. Thy will be done on earth as it is in Heaven. Give us this day, our daily bread. Forgive us our trespasses as we forgive those that have trespassed against us. Lead us not into temptation but deliver us from evil. For Thine is the kingdom the glory forever and ever, Amen. Thank You Jesus, thank You.

Heavenly Father,

I thank You this morning for waking me up and allowing me to get started on my way. Father, You know that I am trying my best to do what I have to do to make it out of here. I don't know who the person or people that is telling things or others to try and discredit me out of my character. Lord in the name of Jesus, I ask that you will reveal them, shame them and send them away from here. Watch over me, keep me out of harms' way and don't let me have to fight for an uncaused reason. You know that I am going to defend myself, I just don't want to be blamed and the snake crawl away. Thank You Lord.

Father God, I thank You, I thank You for my family and friends that has stood by me during this time of my storm. I ask that You will bless each of them according to their hearts. I ask that You will bless my mind and my tongue so that my thoughts and my words will be pleasing unto You. Allow Your light to shine on me so that others will see the beauty of You. May the words I speak be encouraging and up lifting to everyone that I come in contact with.

Heavenly Father, I ask that You will bless each of us in here, our staff members and our families. Watch over all of us as we go to and from. Keep us in the wrath of Your loving arms. In Jesus name I pray. Amen.

Heavenly Father,

I just want to thank You for all that You have done for me. Thank You Lord for all that You are doing for me at this moment. Father, I am so grateful that You are revealing to me all that I need to do to help me get this situation of mine resolved. I could not have done this without You. I am sure that this is my season and all that I have endured is about to work out for the good and that all the Glory belongs to You.

Father God, no matter what my circumstances may be today, I ask that You will bless each of us here in this prison and the staff. Help us to see beauty and light in each one of us. Watch over us and keep us out of harm's way. Father make Yourself known to us in our weakest moments and in our greatest fears. Teach us to receive Your love in a way that enables us to show it to others, especially those closest to us.

Heavenly Father, bless our hearts, our minds, and our tongues so that our thoughts and words are pleasing to You and encouraging to one another. Father, allow Your Holy Spirt to comfort us that are going through doubt, loneliness, missing our families, the loss of our love ones and those of us who just need the assurance of Your Comfort Lord. Reveal Your presence before these young men who even doubt Your existence. I just find it so hard to believe that anyone could even doubt You. Father God my life has not been nothing like I would have wanted it to be, but I am so grateful for all the trials and tribulations, the storms that never seem to end the few joys of life that I have experienced. I know that each one was designed just for me and I am grateful to have survived them all of these years. I know that each second of the minute to the hour, the day, weeks, months and years, You have been there with me and every time I've called out to You that You've heard my every cry. Father God I just want to thank You again for just loving me enough to keep me here. I trust that You will not ever lead me anywhere in which You will leave me and for this I am so very grateful. Father whatever my tomorrows may bring, I just ask that You will give me the strength to finish my journey so I can hear You say "well done, well done my good and faithful servant." Thank You Father, thank You. Our Father, which art in Heaven. Hallowed be thy name. Thy kingdom come, they will be done on earth as it is in Heaven. Give us this day our daily bread and forgive us our trespasses as we forgive those that have trespassed against us. Lead us not into temptation but deliver us from evil. For thine is the kingdom, the glory, the power forever and ever… Amen, amen, amen. Thank You Jesus.

Dear Father God,

Thank You for waking me up this morning and my last night laying down Lord, I thank You for giving me another day to get closer to you.

Father I pray that when You return You will have made me all of what You wanted me to be. I ask now, that you will guide me, show me thy way and teach me Lord. I want to be in the image of You on Judgement Day.

Heavenly Father forgive me for my sins as I have forgiven those that have sinned against me. Lead me not into temptation but deliver me from evil; for Thine is the kingdom, the glory and the power.

Lord bless my thoughts and my words so that they will be pleasing unto You and encouraging to all that I come into contact with. Shine Your light upon me Father so that Your beauty will shine through me. In Jesus name, thank You Lord. Amen.

Made in the USA
Lexington, KY
18 April 2017